W9-AOZ-148

LEVEL 2 READER

OCEAN BABIES

by
Joan Emerson

Scholastic Inc.

PHOTO CREDITS:

Photos ©: cover main: Kevin Schafer Photography; cover driftwood: Stocksolutions/ Dreamstime; back cover: Ingrid Visser/SeaPics.com; 1 main: Kevin Schafer Photography; 1 driftwood: Stocksolutions/Dreamstime; 2 top left and throughout: David Edwards/CG Textures; 2 top right and throughout: Marissa Asuncion; 2 bottom left and throughout: Victorburnside/iStockphoto; 2 bottom right and throughout: Ryhor Bruyeu/Dreamstime; 2-3 background and throughout: nambitomo/ iStockphoto; 3 top: Wild Horizons/UIG via Getty Images; 3 bottom and throughout: FlamingPumpkin/iStockphoto; 4 bubbles and throughout: Wavebreakmedia Ltd/ Thinkstock; 5 top: Hiroya Minakuchi/Minden Pictures/National Geographic Creative; 5 bottom shells and throughout: kyoshino/iStockphoto and David Edwards/CG Textures; 6 top: John C. Lewis/Seapics.com; 6 bottom spiral shells and throughout: Victorburnside/iStockphoto; 9 top: Doug Perrine/SeaPics.com; 9 bottom shells and throughout: Marissa Asuncion; 10 top: beltsazar/Shutterstock, Inc.; 10 bottom shells: Ryhor Bruyeu/Dreamstime; 13: Courtesy Hwa Young Jung; 14: Ingrid Visser/SeaPics. com; 17: Shinji Kusano/Nature Production/Minden Pictures; 18 background: NaluPhoto/iStockphoto; 18 shark: age fotostock/Superstock, Inc.; 21 sand: Wojtek Starak/CG Textures; 21 puffin chick: FLPA/Alamy Images; 22: Hotshotsworldwide/ Dreamstime; 25: Courtesy Sarah Speight; 26: Paul Nicklen/National Geographic Creative; 29 fish: Bruce Coleman Inc./Alamy Images; 29 background: ramihalim/ iStockphoto; 30 sea lion: Susan Flashman/Shutterstock, Inc.; 30 ocean: CG Textures.

Copyright © 2016 by Scholastic Inc.

All rights reserved. Published by Scholastic Inc., *Publishers since 1920.* SCHOLASTIC and associated logos are trademarks and/or registered trademarks of Scholastic Inc.

The publisher does not have any control over and does not assume any responsibility for author or third-party websites or their content.

No part of this publication may be reproduced, stored in a retrieval system, or transmitted in any form or by any means, electronic, mechanical, photocopying, recording, or otherwise, without written permission of the publisher. For information regarding permission, write to Scholastic Inc., Attention: Permissions Department, 557 Broadway, New York, NY 10012.

ISBN 978-0-545-87961-3

Lexile is a registered trademark of MetaMetrics, Inc.

10 9 8 7 6 5 4 3 2 1   16 17 18 19 20 21

Printed in China   68
First printing, January 2016

Designer: Marissa Asuncion
Photo Editor: Emily Teresa

SEA TURTLE

Baby sea turtles, or hatchlings, use a temporary tooth called a caruncle to crack open their eggs. Then, as many as 100 hatchlings work together to dig themselves out of the sand and make their way toward the sea. This can be quite a long walk when you're only a few days old! The baby turtles face so many predators, like birds and crabs, that some scientists believe only 1 in 1,000 survive to adulthood.

Sea turtles were alive at the same time as the dinosaurs, over 200 million years ago!

STINGRAY

Baby stingrays don't have much growing up to do because they're born fully formed! This means that they are born good swimmers and can already find their own food. They have a pointy, sharp stinger, which looks a bit like a tail, and they can use it to defend against predators. Even with this special weapon, stingrays stay close to their mothers until they are 3 years old.

At Stingray City in the Cayman Islands, visitors can swim with stingrays and even feed them!

DOLPHIN

Baby dolphins, also called calves, are some of the smartest babies around. They have great mothers who take care of them until they're 6 years old. Just like humans, dolphin mothers teach their calves everything they know. Still, even great moms get angry sometimes! When mother dolphins feel they are being disobeyed, they head-butt their calves. Ouch!

Dolphins have super-powerful blubber, which can fully heal even after a shark has taken a bite out of it!

SEA HORSE

Sea horse fathers might just earn the "dad of the year" award in this book! Believe it or not, it's the father who becomes pregnant and gives birth to babies. The male sea horse carries up to 2,000 eggs in a special pouch on his stomach for 10 to 25 days. Although the father takes great care of the babies during pregnancy, the **fry** are left on their own within moments of being born.

A sea horse often swims with its tail hooked to another sea horse friend!

HAMMERHEAD SHARK

Baby hammerhead sharks, called **pups**, are usually born in a litter with 12 to 15 other pups. The pups do not get much help from their mothers, so it's a good thing they have so many brothers and sisters! The sharks stay together until they are old enough to set out on their own. When they grow up, they'll hang out in an even bigger group, called a school, with 100 other hammerheads!

A pup's hammer-shaped head helps it see almost 360 degrees around, which means it can see in front, behind, above, *and* below!

PUFFIN

The puffin is a bird that spends nearly its whole life at sea. It uses its wings to swim in the ocean in the same way that it uses them to fly through the air. When it is born, a puffin chick can swim but cannot fly. After a month or so, it spreads its wings and takes flight. It will spend the rest of its days near the ocean, hunting and relaxing on waves when it needs a rest.

The adult puffin is known as the "clown of the sea" because of its bright red beak.

SEA LION

Sea lions might not look like the lion kings of the jungle, but they sure do roar like them! Just like jungle lions, sea lion pups are cared for by their mothers. Before the pups can hunt, it is very important that they drink enough of their mother's milk. This rich milk helps them grow layers of blubber. Many sea lions live in cold water, so they need the blubber to keep them warm!

Sea lions can use their flippers to "walk" on land!

GLOSSARY

blubber: the layer of fat under the skin of a whale, dolphin, or other large marine mammal

calf: the young of several large species of animals, such as dolphins and whales

camouflage: a disguise or a natural coloring that allows animals to hide by making them look like their surroundings

flipper: one of the broad, flat limbs that sea mammals such as seals, whales, and dolphins use when they swim

fry: a baby sea horse

pup: the young of certain animals, like seals, sharks, and sea otters

predator: an animal that hunts other animals for food

salamander: an amphibian that has a tail, like a lizard